Heat of Passion, Rush of Blood

By Nesi Jordan

Dedication

I dedicate this book to my Heavenly Father, Jesus Christ, for granting me the inspiration to create this script in 2006 and for guiding me to revamp it into book form in 2024. To my grandfather, Papa, who passed away in 2010, thank you for giving me the courage to keep writing. I promised myself that I would continue to breathe life into this story, and here it stands—a blend of fiction and non-fiction, reflecting the profound moments that have shaped me.

The part of this story that resonates most deeply with me is when the young lady came to Jesus Christ for a chance to start over, through the unwavering love of her friend. This is a reminder that healthy relationships are the best fruit.

Thank you, J.R., for standing in the gap of prayer for me to return to my spiritual place, which will never end. I love you forever!

1 Corinthians 13:4-7 (NIV)

"Love is patient, love is kind. It does not envy, it does not boast, it is not proud. It does not dishonor others, it is not self-seeking, it is not easily angered, it keeps no record of wrongs. Love does not delight in evil but rejoices with the truth. It always protects, always trusts, always hopes, always perseveres."

Table of Contents

Isaiah 43:18-19 (NIV)

"Forget the former things; do not dwell on the past. See, I am doing a new thing! Now it springs up; do you not perceive it? I am making a way in the wilderness and streams in the wasteland."

Introduction

Welcome to *Heat of Passion, Rush of Blood,* a story born from the depths of my heart and inspired by a journey of faith, love, and redemption.

This book began as a script in 2006, a time when I was exploring the complexities of relationships, the power of forgiveness, and the enduring strength of love. Over the years, this story has evolved, much like the characters within it, into something more profound and spiritually significant. Revamping this work into book form has been a labor of love, fueled by my unwavering faith in Jesus Christ and the memory of my beloved grandfather, Papa, who passed away in 2010. His encouragement and belief in my writing gave me the courage to continue this journey, and I promised myself that I would keep breathing life into this story.

Heat of Passion, Rush of Blood is more than just fiction; it's a blend of real-life experiences and creative storytelling. At its core, it's a reflection of the trials we face in relationships, the importance of healing, and the incredible power of God's love. The famous part of this story, and one that holds a special place in my heart, is the moment when a young woman finds her way back to Christ through the unwavering love and support of a friend who never forgot her. This moment is a testament to the idea that healthy, God-centered relationships are the best kind of fruit we can bear in our lives.

As you read this book, I hope you will see the beauty in second chances, the grace that comes with forgiveness, and the importance of faith in navigating life's challenges. This story is dedicated to those who have ever felt lost, to those who have found their way back, and to everyone who believes in the redemptive power of love.

I also want to take a moment to express my deepest gratitude to J.R., who stood in the gap of prayer for me and helped me return to my spiritual place, a place that will never end. Your support has been invaluable, and I love you forever.

May this book inspire you, comfort you, and remind you that no matter where life takes you, God's love is always there, ready to guide you home.

Blessings,
L.K.J

CHAPTER 1

The Dance of Life

Corinne juggled her shopping bags as she fumbled with her house keys, balancing her cell phone against her ear. The sound of music blaring from within the house made her roll her eyes in exasperation. *Of course, they're having their own little party,* she thought.

As she finally managed to push the door open, she was greeted by the sight of her grandfather, Papa, twirling around the living room, broomstick in hand, belting out lyrics into his makeshift microphone. His graying hair bobbed in time with the music, and his glasses slid down his nose with each exaggerated move. In the kitchen, Memo was humming along, shaking her hips as she tucked away the last of the dishes.

Corinne sighed, letting her shopping bags drop to the floor with a thud. She ended her call and hurried over to the stereo, cutting off the music abruptly. "Papa!" she exclaimed, frustration evident in her voice. "Why didn't you answer the phone?"

Papa paused mid-twirl, a look of genuine confusion crossing his face. "I didn't hear the phone, Cori. I was focusing on my dance aerobics," he explained, resuming his moves despite the silence that now filled the room. "I've got a test in my group tomorrow."

Corinne couldn't help but roll her eyes. *Of all the things...* she thought, though she knew better than to try and interrupt Papa when he was in one of his moods. "I kept calling because I wanted Memo to plug up my curling irons," she said, waving her hands in the air in frustration.

Papa shot her a sarcastic look. "Cori, why are you curling your hair when you could just slap on one of those wigs? Hell, they're already curled," he muttered under his breath, resuming his dance, now without any music to accompany him.

Just then, Memo appeared from the kitchen, her expression sassy as she snatched the broomstick from Papa's grasp. "Does this dance require a broom?" she asked pointedly.

Papa gave her a sharp look, wagging his finger at her. "Hey! If I fail my test, it's going to be *all* your fault," he stressed, his tone playful yet serious.

Corinne glanced at her watch and then back at her grandparents. "Rodney will be here in a minute," she said softly, gathering her shopping bags once more. "Memo, I'll be upstairs."

"Okay, sweetheart," Memo called after her, watching as Corinne ascended the stairs. Once Corinne was out of sight, Memo turned her attention back to Papa. "And as for you, I can already tell you're going to fail that test."

Papa straightened up, mocking indignation. "Look, woman! I would've been a Soul Train dancer if you hadn't called me back in the day saying, 'Hey Harry, my parents aren't going to be home.'" They bickered back and forth like an old married couple, with Memo crossing her arms and rolling her eyes. "If I knew then what I know now," she huffed, "I would've rather polished my toenails."

Their banter was interrupted by the doorbell. Papa pushed his glasses up his nose and pointed his finger at Memo. "Now look here, Minnie..."

The doorbell rang again, and Corinne's voice floated down the stairs, sounding rushed. "Could someone get the door, please?"

Papa opened the door, still glaring at Memo. "You were saved by the bell," he muttered.

Memo, glancing at the door, softened her expression when she saw Rodney standing there. "And you were saved by this child here…. Hello, Rodney baby, how are you doing?" she greeted warmly.

Rodney stepped inside, a strange look on his face as he took in the scene. "Hey, Papa," he nodded respectfully before turning to Memo with a smile. "Hello, Memo. I'm doing fine. Am I interrupting something?"

"No, no, no, baby," Memo reassured him, taking his hand and leading him to the couch. "You know how Papa gets… a little beside himself."

Rodney sat down, tapping his knee nervously as he glanced around. "Is Corinne ready?"

Papa, who had resumed his stretching routine, quipped, "Cori should have been ready. All she had to do was slap that wig on and go."

Memo shot him a disapproving look. "Stop embarrassing that girl," she chided, moving towards the stairs. "Cori baby, Rodney is here!"

Moments later, Corinne appeared at the top of the stairs, looking radiant as she descended. "I'm ready," she announced, smiling at her grandparents. "Papa, good luck on your dance test."

Papa paused his stretching, a grin spreading across his face. "Oh, thank you, baby. At least someone wished me good luck."

Memo patted Papa's shoulder affectionately. "Honey, I'm praying that you get a blessing. Forget luck; you need Jesus," she teased, laughing.

Rodney stood up, clearly impressed as he took Corinne's hand. "You look great!" he exclaimed, unable to hide his awe.

Corinne blushed, returning his smile. "Thank you. So, where are we going tonight?"

Rodney's voice softened, taking on a calm, almost seductive tone. "Well, I was thinking we could go get something to eat and then head back to my place…" He paused, his voice suddenly enthusiastic. "And watch the playoffs!"

Corinne's smile faltered, and she let go of Rodney's hands. "I was hoping we could do something a little different tonight."

Rodney's expression turned worried. "Baby, now you know the playoffs start tonight," he explained, trying to win her over. "And I've got some money riding on these games. Now don't you want to be able to wear Vera Wang?"

Papa, who had been listening from the kitchen, snorted with laughter. "Vera Wang? Hell, Kohl's sells Vera Wang!" he muttered.

Memo elbowed him and placed her finger to her lips, "Shh!"

Corinne looked disappointed but resigned. "Okay, I might as well change my clothes," she sighed.

Rodney's face lit up with relief as he kissed her cheek. "Baby, I knew you would understand. I'll be waiting in the car."

After Rodney left, saying goodbye to Memo and Papa, Corinne trudged upstairs to change. As she did, the phone rang, and Papa, ever the mischief-maker, answered it in his most proper voice, his pipe clutched in hand. "Hello! Harry Fitzgerald speaking."

"Hey, Papa!" came the cheerful voice of Corinne's best friend, Tezah.

Papa's demeanor changed instantly, slipping into a playful Southern drawl. "Who is this?" he asked, feigning confusion as he gestured slyly at Memo, who was trying to figure out who was on the line.

"Tezah," she replied, now confused.

Papa continued his charade. "Who?"

"It's Tezah!" she repeated, a hint of laughter in her voice.

Papa leaned closer to the phone, pretending to whisper loudly. "You just can't be calling here when that old woman is around."

Tezah burst out laughing. "Papa, you're so crazy!"

Papa grinned, walking towards his bedroom with the phone in hand. "So whatcha gon be wearing when you come over? A long skirt, short skirt, no skirt. I know you're just going to let my imagination run wild. I want to know what I'm working with."

Tezah, still playing along, answered innocently, "I was thinking of a short skirt."

Papa's eyebrows shot up. "How short?"

"Oh, Papa, I'll see you when I get there. Bye!" Tezah giggled before hanging up.

Papa continued talking, pretending she was still on the line. "Well, how low can you go, baby? Haha, lardy, lardy, lardy! I was hoping you were going to say that! Umm…"

Just then, Memo appeared in the doorway, holding a kitchen object in her hand, glaring at Papa. "Hey, woman, whatcha doing? That was just Tezah," he protested.

Memo's voice was firm, her eyes narrowed. "I was just about to cash in on your insurance policy."

As Corinne walked back downstairs, Rodney honked the horn outside, yelling, "Cori, come on!"

Taking a deep breath, Corinne shook off the disappointment of the evening and walked out the door, turning off the lights as she left.

Jeremiah 29:11 (NIV)

"For I know the plans I have for you," declares the Lord, "plans to prosper you and not to harm you, plans to give you hope and a future."

CHAPTER 2

The Groove and The Memories

A loud knock echoed through the house, interrupting the silence. Corinne's best friend, Tezah, was at the door, ready to work on a dance assignment. Dressed in a short dance skirt, she unknowingly ignited a spark of youthful mischief in Papa.

Papa shuffled out of his bedroom, grumbling, "Alright, alright, I'm coming. People forget I'm old." But when he opened the door and saw Tezah, his eyes lit up, and he couldn't help but let out a playful wolf whistle.

"Hey Papa, how are you?" Tezah greeted him with a laugh, waving her hand.

Papa, momentarily mesmerized, replied, "Excited... I mean, great!"

Tezah twirled playfully, her skirt swaying as she asked, "Papa, are you ready to get your groove back?"

"Oh yeah, girl, you just put the track in," Papa responded, a spark of youthful energy igniting within him.

Tezah pulled a CD out of her bag and headed toward the radio. "Okay, Papa, I was thinking we should wear solid color outfits..."

Before she could finish, Papa cut her off, rushing to change his clothes. "Yeah, baby, I was thinking the same thing! Wait! I've got just the thing. Let me grab it before we start."

As Tezah began stretching and performing a quick routine to warm up, Papa returned, now clad in a bright yellow spandex suit with shorts over it. He confidently took over the routine, dancing with surprising agility.

Tezah burst into laughter, holding her stomach. "Go, Papa, go Papa!"

Papa dropped to the floor and did the snake, earning even more laughter from Tezah. But just as he was getting into the groove, Memo appeared, turning off the CD and standing over him with a stern look.

"Remember when I said I could tell if you were going to fail?" Memo asked, her hands on her hips.

"Yeah!" Papa replied, quickly.

"You failed," Memo declared sassily, before walking away.

Tezah, still wiping tears of laughter from her face, greeted Memo, "Hey Memo, how are you?"

Memo smiled warmly. "I was doing fine until I walked out here. So, how's the routine going?"

"It's going well," Tezah replied. "But we still have to pick the color for our outfits, and that's proving to be a challenge."

Memo shook Tezah's hand, chuckling. "Good luck, honey, because Harry can't wear everything, as you can see. He's in a class all by himself."

Both women laughed, sharing a knowing glance and a playful hand clap.

Papa, determined not to be outdone, pointed at Memo. "You'll see, Minnie, what I can do."

Memo got in his face and responded, "You're an old man, Harry. Start acting like one!" With that, she walked away.

Papa watched her retreat with a furious look, his frustration palpable. Tezah waved a hand in front of his face to get his attention. "Alright, Papa, I'll see you tomorrow. We're going to do just fine." She placed a reassuring hand on his shoulder, smiling.

Papa snapped back to reality and returned her smile. "Thanks, sweetheart."

As Tezah bent over to put her CD back in her bag, Papa couldn't help but remark, "It's not the gear, it's the rear! My, my, my, my..." He walked her to the door and locked it after she left.

Papa then joined Memo in the living room, sitting next to her, but she ignored him, engrossed in a magazine. He fidgeted, tapping his foot and shifting in his seat, before finally speaking up. "What's wrong with you, Minnie? How come all we do is argue? Sweetheart, we used to have fun back in the day." He stood up and started doing the bump dance by himself, trying to rekindle the spark. "We used to do the bump, the snake, the roll... Well, I've got a lot more to roll now, but that's not the point. We had fun, talk to me, baby!"

Memo lowered the magazine, her face half-hidden behind it. "Yeah, we did have fun, but those days are long gone, Harry."

Papa gently cupped her face in his hands. "We're old, Minnie, but not dead. We can still have fun and love one another... Look at Mom and Pop Winans, Bill and Camille Cosby, or Florida and James Evans... Damn! Damn! Damn!" They both burst into laughter.

Papa continued, his tone more serious. "I remember when we stood outside for the Baker Club auditions. You don't think I remember, but you had on a yellow headband, yellow pumps, two big ole gold hoop earrings, and a yellow and white mini dress." He pulled out a handkerchief, fanning himself as if the memory had heated him up. "Your name went right with that dress... And I don't mean Walt Disney Minnie, if you know what I mean."

Memo allowed herself a small smile. "Yeah, I know what you mean... But Harry, we can't do those things anymore... We are old."

Papa looked at her with deep affection. "Minnie, we're old, but we're not dead. We can still have fun. We can still love each other. You're healed, baby, and you're doing better. Cori and I love and appreciate you. I definitely wouldn't know how to manage without you. God has truly blessed me with a wonderful wife." He then got excited, his tone lightening. "You know what, baby? How about we start planning different things? Let's go to the movies, bowling, or even laser tag!"

Memo cut him off, blushing as she started singing a song called "Angel." "Okay, okay, those sound like good ideas, baby."

With a flirtatious smile, Memo grabbed Papa's hands, leading him towards the bedroom. The song ended as the lights dimmed.

In a high, sexy voice, Memo whispered, "Hey Harry, my parents aren't going to be home."

Papa's voice was full of excitement as he followed her eagerly. "I'm right behind you, baby!"

The room faded to darkness, leaving behind the warmth of rekindled love and the promise of new adventures together.

CHAPTER 3

The Cold Shoulder

The basketball game blared from the television, filling the room with cheers, whistles, and the excited chatter of commentators. Corinne and Rodney sat on the couch in his dimly lit living room. The remnants of their shared popcorn bowl lay empty on the coffee table. Corinne sighed and got up, taking the bowl with her as she headed to the kitchen.

"Thanks, baby, for being so understanding," Rodney murmured, his eyes glued to the screen.

Corinne, feeling the sting of his disinterest, placed her head on Rodney's shoulder, seeking comfort. But instead of reciprocating, Rodney shifted his weight, causing Corinne to nearly fall off the couch.

"Yeah, yeah, whatever makes you happy," Corinne mumbled under her breath as she walked to the kitchen, her frustration growing. She paused at the counter, glancing back at Rodney, who was still engrossed in the game.

"Do you want extra butter and salt on your popcorn?" Corinne asked, trying to keep the irritation out of her voice.

Rodney didn't respond, completely absorbed in the game. The sound of the crowd roaring from the TV drowned out Corinne's question.

"Rodney! Hey, Rodney!" Corinne called out, louder this time.

Rodney, snapping out of his trance, replied with a hint of annoyance. "Yes, baby?"

"Do you want extra butter and salt?" Corinne repeated, her patience wearing thin.

"Yeah, butter and salt," Rodney answered dismissively, his attention already back on the game.

As Corinne reached for the butter, she heard a rhythmic knock at the door—Rodney's cousin Case and his friend Brian had arrived. They entered the house, greeting Corinne with playful enthusiasm.

"Hey, Cooooori!" they chimed in unison, their voices filled with teasing energy.

Corinne barely acknowledged them, rolling her eyes as she shut the door behind them. She felt a growing sense of dread as they made themselves at home.

"What's up, cuzzin?" Case said, giving Rodney a handshake and a hug.

Rodney lit up, thrilled by the arrival of his friends. "What's up, fellas! Sit down. You want a beer? Popcorn?"

Brian accepted a beer while Case grabbed the bowl of popcorn Corinne had just filled.

Corinne, feeling increasingly invisible, leaned over to kiss Rodney on the cheek. "Baby, I'll be in the room," she said, her voice tinged with disappointment.

Rodney barely glanced at her. "Okay, baby..." he replied, his focus never leaving the TV.

As Corinne turned to leave, Brian leaned in toward Rodney. "Is she alright? We could go to the bar, man," he suggested with a laugh.

Rodney brushed it off. "Naw, naw man! She'll be alright." But as Corinne entered the kitchen, Rodney's expression darkened. He followed her, grabbing her by the hair as soon as they were out of sight.

"What's wrong with you, huh? You getting a little beside yourself, getting mad for what?" he hissed, his voice low and threatening. "Why don't you call Tezah on the new cell phone I bought you?"

Corinne winced in pain, tears welling up in her eyes. "Rodney, you're hurting me... What are you doing? Stop it!" she cried, her voice trembling.

From the living room, Case and Brian glanced back toward the kitchen, sensing the tension.

"What y'all love birds doing? You're missing a good game, man!" Case called out, his tone half-joking.

Rodney quickly composed himself, forcing a smile as he turned to his friends. "We cool, brah!" he replied. Then, lowering his voice, he whispered harshly to Corinne, "Shut up! You're embarrassing me. Just go to the room now!"

Corinne, heartbroken and shaken, ran to the bedroom. She threw herself on the bed and, with tears streaming down her face, grabbed her phone to call her best friend, Tezah.

Meanwhile, Rodney returned to the couch, greeting his friends as if nothing had happened. "Alright, fellas, what did I miss?"

In the bedroom, Corinne wiped her tears and dialed Tezah's number. "Hey, T, what are you doing?" she asked, trying to steady her voice.

"Hola, mommie! I just left your house. Girl! Yo papa..." Tezah started, but Corinne cut her off.

"Tezah, don't even go there... say no more. Did you all finish the routine yet?"

"Yeah, we finished. Girl, do you know Papa wants to wear a tight-fitted, yellow suit to dance in?" Tezah burst into laughter.

Corinne couldn't help but join in. "What! Girl, bye! I believe it, I believe it. Papa is a character that only he could play."

"Right!! So, where are you? Over Rodney's?"

"Girl, yes, and you already know…" Corinne sighed.

"He got company!" they both said in unison, laughing despite the situation.

"I thought y'all were going out to a nice restaurant and the Oasis?" Tezah asked, her tone turning serious.

"Change of plans. I guess it slipped his mind," Corinne replied, the hurt evident in her voice.

"Well, check this out. I got this book called *Give Me Time*. It's a good read, even though I've only gotten to the second chapter."

"What's it about?" Corinne asked, curious.

"It's a 40-day adventure about noticing spiritual men who love their women," Tezah explained.

Corinne, needing a distraction, perked up. "Tezah, where are you at right now?"

"At home, why?"

"'Cause, child, I need that book."

Tezah laughed. "Girl, you can borrow it. I'm done with it. All it's doing is sitting here collecting dust."

"I'm on my way. Girl, bye!" Corinne said, feeling a surge of determination.

"Okay, sweetie, bye!" Tezah responded, still amused. Corinne hung up the phone, resolving to find some solace in the pages of the book. She grabbed her purse and, after trying to get Rodney's attention one last time, decided it was pointless. She waved her hand in a final attempt, but he was too engrossed in the game to notice.

"Rodney, I'll see you later," she called out, but Rodney was too absorbed to respond. Corinne walked out the door, the sound of Rodney and his friends cheering and hollering in the background. As she stepped outside, the cold air hit her, and she felt a strange sense of relief wash over her. The door clicked shut behind her, and she took a deep breath, her heart heavy but her spirit resolute. The night was quiet, the streetlights casting long shadows as she walked toward her car. Alone in the darkness, Corinne began to sing softly, a melancholy tune that echoed her feelings of loneliness and longing. Her voice carried through the still night air, a quiet testament to her strength as she drove away, seeking comfort in the words of a book and the promise of something better.

CHAPTER 4

The Dance Exam

The dance studio buzzed with anticipation as everyone stretched and chatted, glancing at the large mirror that lined the front wall. This was the moment they had all been preparing for—their final dance exam. Papa, as usual, was brimming with a mix of excitement and mischief.

Ms. Reese entered the room with her usual air of authority, ready to start the day. "Good morning, everyone," she greeted, her voice firm yet warm. "Are we ready for our final exam?" She paused, surveying the room. "Well then... let's get started. I wanted to change things up a bit today."

She walked to the front of the room, pulling out a small hat. "We're going to draw numbers to determine the order of the dances. Let's see who's first."

The dancers approached one by one, each pulling a number from the hat. A little boy rushed ahead, nearly knocking into Papa, who glared down at him in annoyance.

"Which group is first?" Ms. Reese asked, ready to begin.

A girl in the front raised her hand eagerly. "We are!" she called out.

"Alright then," Ms. Reese said, nodding. "Who's group two?"

Before anyone could answer, Papa pointed accusingly at the little boy. "Well, we would have been if this lil crumb snacker hadn't cut in front of us."

The little boy turned and gave Papa a defiant shake of his head, which only fueled Papa's irritation.

"Mr. Fitzgerald, let it go," Ms. Reese instructed, trying to keep the situation under control.

"But… but…" Papa began to protest.

"Let it go," Ms. Reese repeated, more firmly this time. "Relax, relate, and release. Now, group one, take the floor."

Group one performed their routine with energy and precision, earning applause from the class. Ms. Reese made a few notes in her grade book. "Good, very good. Group two, you're up next."

As group two began to move into position, Papa couldn't resist a final act of mischief and tried to trip the little boy. The boy shot him a frustrated look and turned to Ms. Reese. "Ms. Reese! Would you tell this grown man to stop?"

"Mr. Fitzgerald, please!" Ms. Reese scolded. "That's a little boy. Come on, group two, let's get started."

As the little boy stuck his tongue out at Papa, Papa leaned over to Tezah, whispering, "You see what he just did? Damien, just pure evil."

Tezah tried to shush Papa, knowing Ms. Reese's patience was wearing thin. "Papa, stop it," she whispered urgently. "Look, they're good."

"We are too," Papa muttered, determined not to be outdone.

Tezah clapped her hands, signaling it was their turn. "Okay, let's show them what we've got."

As they performed their routine, Papa gave it his all, his energy contagious. When the music finally stopped, he cupped his hands around his mouth and shouted, "What's the grade, huh? What's the grade, baby?!"

Tezah looked at Papa in shock, her admiration for his talent clear. "Papa, you've got talent," she said, genuinely impressed.

Papa grinned, imitating Ray Charles. "I do what I do, baby!"

Ms. Reese smiled as she made the final entries in her grade book. "Alright, class, I was going to wait to give you your grades, but since everyone did so well, here you go."

Group one jumped up in excitement, showing off their papers to each other. "Wow!" they exclaimed.

Group two quietly accepted their papers, nodding in satisfaction. Papa craned his neck, trying to see what they got.

"What did you get?" Papa asked the little boy, his curiosity getting the better of him.

The little boy smirked and stepped on Papa's foot. "None of your business!" he shouted before dashing off.

Papa bristled and shook his fist after him. "Boy, I will take this belt off!" he threatened.

Ms. Reese handed Papa and Tezah their grade. "Here you go, Mr. Fitzgerald."

Tezah eagerly looked at their paper. "We got an A-minus."

Papa adjusted his glasses and peered at the grade. "An A-minus? Wait a minute… A minus? How did we—"

Ms. Reese held up her hand, stopping him mid-sentence. "Have a good day, Mr. Fitzgerald."

Papa wasn't ready to let it go. "You know what…" he started, ready to argue.

But Tezah quickly grabbed his arm, steering him towards the door. "Let's go, Papa. Let's go celebrate!"

Papa mumbled under his breath as they walked out, still grumbling about the unfair grade. "Yeah, right… celebrate."

The lights dimmed as they exited, leaving the echoes of their performance and Papa's gripes hanging in the air.

CHAPTER 5

Burning Bridges

Corinne had just stepped out of a relaxing bubble bath, feeling refreshed. She settled into her bed, flipping through the pages of a book titled *Forty Days Adventure of Time*, a Christian guide aimed at fostering spiritual growth. As she read, she came across a series of introspective questions designed to provoke deep thought.

"First, are you saved?" Corinne mused aloud. "Yes. Second, are you ready to surrender to God?" She hesitated, her finger resting on her chin. "I've thought about it... What's the next question? 'Are you practicing abstinence?' Well... That's why Tezah stopped on day two."

Just as she set the book aside, her phone buzzed with an incoming call. It was Rodney.

"Hola!" Corinne answered, not bothering to check the caller ID.

"Hey, baby! How are you? How come you didn't say you were leaving..." Rodney's voice came through, cheerful yet insistent.

Corinne's frustration bubbled up. "Wait! Wait! You're calling me the next day to ask why I didn't say I was leaving? That game must have been really important."

Rodney tried to smooth things over. "It was. I got some good money coming in from the fellas at work. Plus, I admit I was mad and had a few too many drinks… and passed out."

A sigh escaped Corinne's lips. "You know what? Bye, Rodney."

"Cori!!" Rodney's voice was desperate now.

"Goodnight, Rodney!" Corinne replied, her tone mocking as she yawned. "I'm about to pass out."

"Cori, Corinne… Hello? Baby, listen, we could do something tomorrow. How about going to the Oasis? We both can get massages. You know you'll love that…"

Corinne cut him off sharply. "Rodney, you've put me on the back burner for a long time now, and I'm sick of it. I make time for you, but you never think about me and how I might feel. You disrespect me and say you love me." She stood up, her voice gaining strength. "I want to be more appreciated, not just as your girlfriend but as a woman! So it's more like when you have time. Goodbye!"

Rodney's frustration boiled over. "Hold on! Hold on! When you wanted to go to those boring stage plays, I went! When you wanted to take long walks and have picnics in the park, I went! I've bought you whatever you wanted and needed. Things you couldn't even pronounce! So don't tell me I don't care. What else do you want from me, huh? Come outside."

Corinne looked out the window, her voice cold and firm. "Leave my house, Rodney. As for the boring things, your body was there, but your mind was somewhere else. You don't have time, and I don't either. I'm tired of this unnecessary bull! That was the last time you put your hands on me! And as for you buying me things… listen." She began to sing, her voice full of resolve.

Rodney's anger reached its peak. "What, you're breaking up with me?"

Corinne's response was clear and confident. "I guess so. Sorry." She hung up the phone and walked away from the window.

Rodney, throwing a tantrum, shouted, "Naw, naw, you're mine! Breaking up with me? You ain't going nowhere!" His anger was palpable as he sang out his frustration.

A woman pushing a baby stroller passed by Rodney as he threw his fit. She paused, soothing her fussy baby.

"Shh! Baby, we're almost home. Are you okay, sir?" she asked.

Rodney, now calming down and getting off the ground, replied, "Yeah, I'm fine. I just have a lot going on. My girlfriend just broke up with me."

The woman, covering her baby with a blanket, offered advice. "Maybe you should ask the Lord for some guidance. I can see you have a lot of anger in you, and that type of behavior will only make you sick. Get yourself together and calm down. Send her some flowers." As the baby fussed again, she added, "I've got to go... Young man, take care."

With that, the scene fades out, the lights dimming as the focus shifts to the flower shop.

Romans 8:28 (NIV)

"And we know that in all things God works for the good of those who love him, who have been called according to his purpose."

CHAPTER 6

Flower's Blooming

At First Love Florist, the rhythmic sound of the shop's bell chimed as customers came and went. Inside, L.J., an energetic employee, was juggling orders and phone calls. The atmosphere was busy yet controlled, until the urgent ring of his phone disrupted the usual cadence.

His Uncle Troy's voice crackled through the receiver, tinged with urgency and distress.

"Hey L.J., your wife is in labor! You need to get here right now. She's squeezing the life out of my hand!" Uncle Troy's voice was strained. L.J. could hear Lisa's pained cries in the background.

"I'm on my way, I'm on my way!" L.J. said, hanging up swiftly. He turned to Joshua Keeps, the shop's owner, who was preparing for the evening's church revival.

Joshua, dressed sharply in a cream suit, had just finished a call with his pastor. He was about to head out when he noticed L.J.'s frazzled state.

"Yo, L.J., you're looking fly!" Joshua greeted, giving his friend a fist bump.

L.J., trying to maintain his composure, replied, "Thanks, man. I've got to run an errand. Marvin's already gone for the day, and we have one more delivery. Can you handle it?"

Joshua, eager to help, nodded. "Of course! Get to your wife. I've got this."

"Thanks, dawg. The roses are ready, and I appreciate your encouragement. Have a good night! I'm about to be a dad!" L.J. said with a burst of excitement as he rushed out the door.

Joshua gathered the flower arrangement, feeling a surge of emotions. As he prepared to leave, he whispered a silent prayer, thanking God for the blessings in his life and for the future he hoped to build.

The scene shifted as Joshua drove to Corinne's house, the quiet suburban streets giving way to a more personal moment. He rang the doorbell and knocked, glancing at his watch, aware of the ticking clock.

A few moments later, the door creaked open, and Corinne appeared, her eyes widening in surprise.

"Hey, wait! Are those flowers for me?" she asked, glancing at Joshua with curiosity.

"Yes, ma'am," Joshua replied, holding out the bouquet.

Corinne's eyes widened as she took in Joshua's appearance. "Wow! I've never seen a delivery man look this sharp."

Joshua smiled warmly. "Actually, I'm the owner of First Love Florist."

"Joshua? Is that really you?" Corinne asked, her face lighting up with recognition.

"Yes, it's me. It's been a long time since high school. You look great," Joshua said, his voice filled with genuine warmth.

Corinne's cheeks flushed slightly. "Thank you. So, you own the shop now?"

Joshua nodded. "Yes, my father passed away a year after we graduated. He left me the shop, and I've been running it since."

"I'm sorry to hear about your father," Corinne said sympathetically. "He was a sweet man. I don't mean to be rude, but would you like to come in for a moment? If you have time."

Joshua accepted the invitation, stepping inside and removing his hat. "I didn't realize you lived here. What happened? Why the move to this quiet part of town?"

Corinne placed the flowers in a vase and sighed. "My mom was murdered. The police found her body in pieces, left in a dumpster not far from our old home. After graduation, I moved here to live with my grandparents."

Joshua's face softened with compassion as he embraced Corinne, who was beginning to break down. Through her tears, she shared memories of her mother and the emotional weight of her loss.

"I'm so sorry, Cori. Why didn't you reach out to me?" Joshua asked, his voice filled with concern.

Corinne wiped her tears and managed a sad smile. "I didn't want to hurt you further. But I'm okay now. I cherish the good memories from before things changed."

Joshua's eyes widened in surprise. "Your mom was involved in...?"

"Yes," Corinne said quietly. "She was."

Joshua shook his head, remembering the strong, supportive woman he'd known. "She always emphasized finishing school and staying true to ourselves."

They shared a nostalgic laugh, recalling the simple yet cherished moments of their youth. Joshua's phone rang, breaking the moment.

"Excuse me, Cori," he said, checking the caller ID. "I need to take this call."

"Sure," Corinne replied, watching as Joshua answered.

Joshua spoke briefly on the phone, explaining that the call was from his pastor, needing him to retrieve some items forgotten at home. As he ended the call, Corinne's curiosity got the better of her.

"I didn't mean to keep you from your wife and children," she said, feeling a bit awkward.

Joshua smiled. "Oh, I'm not married or have any children. That was my pastor calling. He's in a bind and needed me to pick up some things."

"Wow, you must have a great relationship with your pastor," Corinne said, clearly impressed.

Joshua nodded. "He's been like a spiritual father to me. After high school, when I was struggling with so many losses, including you leaving, my father passing away, and falling into the wrong crowd, I found solace in my faith. My pastor's guidance was instrumental in my journey."

Corinne's eyes softened, touched by Joshua's story. "I appreciate you sharing that. It's good to see you again."

Joshua took her hand gently. "It was really good seeing you, Cori. If you're interested, the church revival is tonight. Maybe you could come."

Corinne hesitated, glancing down at her casual attire. "I don't have anything to wear."

Joshua chuckled. "It's come as you are—both your clothes and your heart. You could ride with me if you'd like."

Corinne hesitated for a moment, then shook her head with a laugh. "I think I'll stay in and finish my book. Maybe next time."

Joshua smiled, understanding her reluctance. "Alright, but if you change your mind, it starts at 6 p.m., just five blocks away at Great Lakes Head Start Church."

As Joshua prepared to leave, Corinne's phone buzzed with a new message. She glanced at it, reading Rodney's threatening voicemail. Concern crossed her face as she realized she needed to escape the situation.

"I'm going to that revival," she decided, rushing to her room to change clothes. Joshua watched her with a hopeful smile before stepping out of the house.

As Corinne hurried to get ready, she felt a spark of hope and determination. The revival might just be the beginning of a new chapter in her life.

CHAPTER 7

Divine Love

Joshua entered the church, the air thick with the summer heat. Fans fluttered in the congregation, struggling to combat the stifling warmth. He made his way to the front, where the First Lady awaited. With a smile, he handed her the forgotten items—a black purse, a gold watch, and two baby bottles.

"Thank you, Joshua," she said, taking the items gratefully. Joshua nodded, turning his attention to the Pastor, who had just stepped up to the pulpit.

"Good evening, saints," the Pastor began, his voice resonant and commanding. "I have an announcement to make. There's a baby blue Volkswagen with the license plate 'TICKLE ME PINK.' Your lights are on."

A man in the congregation stood up, mumbling, "That's my sister's car."

"Okay," the Pastor responded quickly. "Meanwhile, back at the ranch, this is our 2nd Annual Great Lakes Head Start Church Revival, and we have a special message for you all that is going to bless you. Amen, saints?"

The congregation responded with a hearty, "Amen!"

"Sister Perry is going to bless us with a song," the Pastor continued. "Then we're going to hear some testimonies. We only have time for two, although everyone has something to share about the goodness of the Lord. Alright, Sister Perry, you can come up now."

Sister Perry approached the pulpit with a smile, and her voice soon filled the room with a beautiful melody. The congregation responded with applause and amens, their spirits lifted by the heartfelt performance.

"Amen, amen," the Pastor said, his eyes shining. "That was beautiful, Sister Perry, just beautiful. Now we will hear two testimonies."

A woman in a wheelchair was the first to share. "Thank you, Jesus, for blessing me," she said, her voice full of gratitude. "I never thought I would be in this situation, but I just thank God!"

The Pastor leaned in, whispering, "Lena, what are you doing?"

The First Lady stood up, a determined look on her face. "Charles, I have to do this," she said. She turned to the congregation, her voice steady. "Let me tell you how good God is. This was four years before Pastor and I got married..." She began recounting her story, her testimony both touching and inspiring.

The Pastor wrapped his arms around her, his eyes glistening with love and pride. "Thank you, Jesus, for blessing me with this beautiful woman," he said, his voice choked with emotion. "If you're looking for a church home and want to have a closer walk with the Lord, please come. Please come."

As the choir began to sing, the Pastor and the First Lady retreated to the church office to console one another, their bond evident and strong. Joshua took to the pulpit, offering the closing prayer as the service came to a close.

After the service, Corinne approached Joshua, her eyes bright with resolve. "I want to be baptized," she said, her voice steady. "I'm ready to live right."

Joshua looked at her, surprised. "Cori, are you sure?"

"I want to feel loved again," Corinne said, her voice filled with longing. "I want my life back."

Joshua embraced her warmly. "Wait right here. Let me go get the Pastor."

The Pastor returned quickly, his demeanor both welcoming and encouraging. "So you want to be saved, huh? That's so good to know. You can be saved right now. The first Sunday, you will be baptized. Is that okay?" He looked at Corinne with kind eyes. "In Romans 10:9, it speaks about confessing with your mouth and believing in your heart that Jesus is Lord. Do you love the Lord? Do you believe that Jesus died on the cross and rose from the dead?"

Corinne nodded, her voice soft but firm. "Yes."

"There you go, young lady," the Pastor said with a smile. "You are saved. We welcome you to The Great Lakes Head Start Church family."

The First Lady's baby began to cry. "Okay, family, that's my cue to go home," she said, rocking the stroller.

"Okay, First Lady," Joshua said, giving her a nod. "I'll see you in the morning."

"In the morning?" she responded, surprised. "Joshua, what are you talking about?"

"Remember the kiddie bake sale here at the church?" Joshua reminded her.

"Oh, that's right," the First Lady said, recalling the event. "Nice to meet you, Corinne. Welcome to the family, and Joshua, goodbye."

Joshua turned to Corinne with a smile. "So, Cori, did you enjoy yourself? It's so great to be saved, and you know what else? I'm grateful to be a part of this gift you experienced."

Corinne and Joshua shared a moment, their eyes locking in mutual understanding. Then Corinne checked the time, her expression turning to concern.

"Well," she said, "I forgot about my papa celebrating his dance grade. I'm late. So, I'll talk to you later. Thank you so much."

Joshua gave her a warm hug. "Okay, I'll see you. Maybe we can get some lunch one day next week?"

Corinne smiled. "I'd like that. Sounds like a deal."

Joshua started to clean up, humming a tune as he gathered his things. He noticed Corinne's sweater and phone left behind. "She left her sweater and phone," he said with a chuckle, sniffing the sweater. "I'll have to take this to her."

He turned off the lights and locked up, looking forward to their next meeting and feeling a deep sense of satisfaction.

CHAPTER 8

Unexpected Visitors

The house was alive with celebration as Papa, Memo, and Tezah gathered around a table adorned with a rich, double chocolate cake. The atmosphere was festive, and the chatter was filled with joy and laughter as they celebrated Tezah's latest dance grade.

Tezah, slicing into the cake with a look of contentment, glanced around the room with a hint of concern. "It's such a blessing that we can celebrate in peace," she said. "Where is Cori? I thought she would have been here by now."

Papa, who was savoring each bite of his cake, shrugged nonchalantly. "Well, you know how Cori is… she's probably at the mall, matching wigs with her shoes."

Memo, rifling through some papers, picked up a note and read aloud. "Baby, stop… Cori went to a church revival. Here's the note."

Papa and Tezah exchanged puzzled looks. "Church?" Papa echoed, raising an eyebrow. "They must be selling purses."

Tezah chuckled. "Well, good people, I'm out of here. I've got to get up early for work."

Papa, looking up from his cake with a grin, asked, "Are you going to keep it? Where do you work now? Every week it's a different job."

Tezah rolled her eyes playfully. "Kept Secrets at the mall."

Papa's eyes widened in surprise. "What!! Don't get smart, lil' girl…"

Memo, sensing the shift in the conversation, interjected to steer it back. "Harry, remember that lace I brought home for our romantic evening?"

Papa's face lit up with recognition. "Oh, oh, oh yes, that red and touch of gold see-through…"

Memo cut him off with a playful smirk. "Okay, okay, Harry, that's enough… that's the place where Tezah works."

Papa, giving Tezah a light push toward the door, said, "Yeah, you go so the doors can be opened bright and early! I definitely will be investing more money so you will forever have a job, child."

Tezah laughed. "Love you guys… tell Cori I'll talk to her later. Thanks."

Memo covered the cake with a flourish. "Harry, I love you and I've got a surprise for you!"

Papa's curiosity was piqued. "I love you too, baby… what's the surprise? You got another Kept Secret?"

Memo grinned mischievously. "Just wait and see."

Papa, still intrigued, headed towards the kitchen. "Okay, baby, let me get a glass of milk and I'll be right there." He looked up, adding with a touch of humor, "Lord have mercy, this woman is going to be the death of me. Thank you, Jesus, for my family."

Memo called out, "Harry!!"

Papa pointed up to the ceiling. "Here I come, baby!!!" and headed into the bedroom.

Meanwhile, Corinne set her purse down with a sigh of relief. "Wow, I'm saved," she murmured to herself. "Let me call Tezah." Her gaze fell on the empty space where her cell phone usually rested. "Oh no, I forgot my cell at the church." She grabbed her purse and opened the front door just as Joshua knocked.

"Hey, you forgot your sweater and cell phone," Joshua said, holding up the items with a friendly smile.

Corinne opened the door wider, inviting him in. "I was just so excited… Come in for a minute, excuse the mess."

Joshua stepped inside, glancing around with an appreciative nod. "Your grandparents had a big celebration."

Corinne nodded, slicing the cake. "Yeah… would you like some? It's double chocolate."

Joshua's face brightened. "Yeah, sure… Hey, Cori, could I use your restroom?"

"Sure… It's the second door down the hall," Corinne replied, pointing towards the hallway.

Just as Joshua was about to head to the restroom, a loud, aggressive knock echoed through the house. Corinne's heart sank as she saw Rodney standing at the door, his stance unsteady and a bottle of liquor in hand.

"Rodney, what do you want? You need to leave," Corinne said, her voice tinged with unease. "It's getting late, and you're drunk."

Rodney, swaying slightly, pushed the door open and staggered inside. "Dang, baby, it's like that? I just wanted to talk to you…" He licked icing off his finger, smirking as he eyed the cake. "Double chocolate, my favorite."

"No, Rodney," Corinne said firmly, stepping back. "You need to leave now. You're drunk and you stink…"

Joshua, emerging from the restroom, dried his hands and took in the tense scene. Rodney's gaze shifted toward him with a sudden, hostile intensity. Without warning, Rodney lunged at Joshua, reaching for his throat. A scuffle broke out, and Corinne screamed as she tried desperately to pull Rodney off Joshua. The situation escalated rapidly, with lights flickering as Corinne was accidentally elbowed and fell to the floor.

Joshua, dropping to his knees beside Corinne, his face etched with worry, said urgently, "Cori, are you okay?" He fumbled for his cell phone and quickly dialed. "Yes, we have an emergency at 310 March Place. A woman is hurt and unconscious. Please hurry!" His voice was a mix of panic and determination. "They're on their way. Cori, hold on… hold on."

Rodney, realizing the severity of the situation, mumbled an apology. "I'm sorry… I'm sorry," before rushing out the door, leaving a trail of chaos in his wake.

Papa and Memo, alerted by the commotion, burst from the bedroom with concern etched on their faces. "Cori, baby… What happened?" Memo's voice was laced with panic as she knelt beside Corinne.

Within minutes, the police and EMS arrived, their sirens cutting through the night. They quickly assessed the scene, asked a flurry of questions, and prepared to transport Corinne. The once joyful celebration had turned into a somber scene of uncertainty and worry. The room was filled with the sounds of hurried footsteps and urgent voices as the emergency personnel worked diligently to provide aid.

As Corinne was carefully placed on a stretcher and wheeled out of the house, the weight of the night's events hung heavily in the air. The celebration was forgotten, replaced by a profound sense of dread and concern for Corinne's well-being.

CHAPTER 9

A Miracle of Faith

The sterile scent of antiseptic filled the hospital corridor as Joshua paced nervously. The waiting area was hushed, punctuated only by the occasional murmur of other concerned families. Joshua's heart was heavy with worry, but he remained hopeful. Corinne's grandparents, Memo and Papa, sat nearby, their faces etched with concern and fatigue.

Dr. Shane entered the waiting room with a calm, professional demeanor. His appearance, though authoritative, radiated reassurance. "Hello, I'm Dr. Shane. Are you Corinne Fitzgerald's husband?"

Joshua, his voice tinged with sadness, shook his head. "No, ma'am. I'm a close friend."

Memo, standing beside Papa, stepped forward. "We're Corinne's grandparents, Doctor."

Papa, his hands trembling slightly, looked at Dr. Shane with a mixture of hope and fear. "Doctor Shane, is my granddaughter going to die?"

Dr. Shane offered a reassuring smile. "No, no, sir. Corinne's vitals are stable, and she's going to be just fine. She has a minor concussion, but she's very fortunate that the ambulance arrived quickly. It could have been much worse. The cut was small, and we've stitched it up. She should wake up in a couple of hours. What actually happened?"

Joshua, still shaken, recounted the events. "Corinne's ex-boyfriend, Rodney, attacked me. She tried to intervene, and he elbowed her pretty hard. She fell into the table, and that's when I called for the ambulance."

Nurse Janis, who had been quietly observing, approached. "I overheard. Corinne must really care about you to jump in between two men like that. What she needs now is rest and lots of love when she wakes up. Any questions?"

Memo, her voice breaking slightly, replied, "No, Doctor. We just thank you so much."

Papa, wiping a tear from his eye, shook Dr. Shane's hand. "Thanks, Doctor."

Dr. Shane nodded. "You folks enjoy your night."

Nurse Janis glanced at her watch and then at the clock on the wall. "I'm sorry, but visiting hours will be over in three minutes. Corinne needs her rest. We'll call you first thing in the morning."

Papa, frustrated, protested, "What? We just got here."

Memo, trying to calm the situation, added, "We wanted to be here when Cori woke up."

Nurse Janis remained polite but firm. "I understand, but there's a family waiting room down the hall. Doctor Shane's orders are for Corinne to rest without interruptions."

Papa, his voice rising, grumbled, "I don't understand this. Some bull—"

Memo interrupted, her tone gentle but firm. "Harry, let's go. We'll be in the waiting room. Harry, shhh!" She guided him toward the hallway.

Joshua, with a sense of urgency, approached Nurse Janis. "Excuse me, Nurse Janis. Could I have a minute with Corinne?"

Nurse Janis raised an eyebrow, intrigued. "Are you her husband?"

Joshua, his voice soft and hopeful, answered, "No. Hopefully, someday she will be my wife."

Nurse Janis's smile widened. "I overheard what happened. You must really care for her if you're willing to wait. If it's in the Lord's plan, it shall happen." She checked her watch. "One minute."

Joshua nodded, feeling a surge of emotion. He entered Corinne's room, where her tranquil face lay against the pillow. He clasped her hand gently, his voice filled with sincerity. "Corinne, I know you can hear me. This is Joshua. I've loved you since high school. We thought our feelings were just a youthful fling, but as we grew, I realized that my heart had never truly let go of you."

Tears formed in his eyes as he continued. "I thought about you in every relationship I had. I looked for pieces of you in them, but they were never enough. I love you, Corinne. I remember our letters and the promise we made to reunite someday. That day is now. I need you to wake up. I want to hear your voice and see your smile."

He took a deep breath, invoking his faith. "Lord, Your Word in 1 Corinthians 13 speaks of love being patient and kind, not envious or boastful. It's a mature love that shines bright in the darkest times. I pray that Your love envelops Corinne, and that we may share this love in Your light."

Nurse Janis, stepping back into the room, gently cleared her throat. "Sir, time is up."

Joshua leaned in, kissing Corinne's hand tenderly. "I'll see you when you wake up. I'll be just down the hall."

As Joshua exited the room, he made his way to the hospital chapel. Kneeling in prayer, he poured out his heart to God. "Lord, I've prayed for Corinne and our future together. Please allow her to wake up and receive the full blessings You have promised. I promise to cherish her and our life together."

Outside the chapel, Nurse Janis watched as Joshua walked to the waiting room. Her gaze softened with understanding.

Suddenly, a frantic cry echoed through the hospital corridors. "Joshua! Joshua!"

Joshua sprinted back to Corinne's room, where he found her eyes open, her face streaked with tears. "Get off him, Rodney! Are you okay, Joshua?" she asked, embracing him tightly. "I was trying to find my way back to you. Everything was dark except for you and me. I followed the light, and there you were."

Tears of relief and joy streamed down Joshua's face. "I'm here, Corinne. I'm here."

Memo and Papa, who had been anxiously waiting, rushed into the room. Memo, her voice choked with emotion, said, "Cori, we love you. Memo's here, baby."

Papa, his eyes misty, hugged Corinne tightly. "Cori, I'm glad you're okay."

Nurse Janis approached to check Corinne's vitals, reminding her of the need for rest. "You still need your rest. Let me check your vitals."

Corinne smiled weakly, gratitude evident in her eyes. "Thank you so much... Thank you, God."

As Nurse Janis finished, she said, "God sends His angels to be the vehicle, and He is the driver. Get some rest, sweetie."

The scene shifted to Corinne leaving the hospital, her recovery marked by the love and support surrounding her. Joshua was there every step of the way, his dedication unwavering.

Papa, trying to lighten the mood, joked, "Cori, I would have missed your different wigs just that quickly."

Memo playfully scolded him. "Shut up, Harry. Stop embarrassing that girl."

Corinne shook her head with a smile. "Here they go again... Welcome to the family."

Joshua took Corinne's hand and kissed it tenderly. "I love you and them."

In a moment of pure joy, Joshua bent down on one knee, proposing to Corinne. The soft music playing in the background, coupled with the beaming smiles of Papa and Memo, made the moment unforgettable. Rodney was nowhere in sight, having left town, allowing the focus to remain on the couple's joy.

"Everyone says there are no good men out here," Corinne reflected, her voice filled with emotion. "But God says that he who finds a wife finds a good thing."

As their love story continued, Joshua and Corinne faced new chapters with faith and optimism. They eagerly anticipated the arrival of their first child together. Corinne, who had children from a previous relationship, and Joshua, who had only godchildren, were overjoyed at the news. The prospect of becoming parents filled their hearts with profound happiness and purpose.

Joshua's health remained a concern, with his pacemaker, and lung disease being constant reminders of his vulnerability. Yet, with Corinne by his side, he felt a renewed sense of hope and determination. Their love for each other, their unwavering faith in Jesus Christ, and the excitement of their growing family marked the beginning of a new and blessed chapter in their lives.

As they prepared for their baby's arrival, their story became a testament to the power of love, faith, and the divine blessings that come from trusting in God's plan.

CHAPTER 10

Family Announcement

The evening sun cast a golden glow over Corinne and Joshua's home, setting the stage for a memorable family gathering. The living room was meticulously arranged with a delightful spread of food and elegant decorations. In the center of the table lay a small, wrapped gift, chosen with care by Corinne as a special way to announce their joyous news.

Joshua sat beside Corinne, his hand resting gently on hers. The love and anticipation in his eyes were unmistakable. Their hearts were full as they prepared to share the incredible news of their twins with their close family.

Memo and Papa arrived, their excitement evident. Memo's eyes sparkled with curiosity, while Papa, ever the jester, made light-hearted comments about hoping the gift wasn't another kitchen gadget.

"Alright, everyone," Corinne said, her voice trembling with both excitement and nervousness. "Joshua and I have something special to share with you."

Memo and Papa exchanged intrigued glances as Corinne carefully handed over the wrapped gift. With a sense of ceremony, Memo unwrapped the package, revealing a framed ultrasound photo of the twins. The room fell silent as the significance of the image registered.

"What is this?" Memo asked, her voice barely a whisper as she held the photo up for everyone to see.

"It's our little announcement," Corinne replied, her eyes glistening with tears of joy. "We're having twins!"

The room erupted into joyful noise. Memo's hand flew to her mouth in astonishment, and Papa's eyes filled with tears of happiness. They embraced Corinne and Joshua, their excitement and love palpable.

"This is wonderful news!" Memo exclaimed, her voice choked with emotion. "Congratulations, both of you!"

Papa, always the emotional one, had tears streaming down his face. "I'm so happy for you, Cori. And Joshua, you're going to be a fantastic father."

As they celebrated, Corinne and Joshua felt a deep sense of gratitude. They knew that their journey had been blessed by God's grace. Each moment of joy was a testament to their faith and His unwavering support.

Before the evening ended, Corinne and Joshua gathered their family for a moment of prayer. "Heavenly Father," Joshua began, his voice filled with reverence, "we thank You for the incredible blessing of these twins. We acknowledge Your hand in every step of our journey and give You all the glory. May these children grow in Your love and grace."

Amen.

The room was filled with a profound sense of peace and gratitude as the family continued to celebrate, knowing that their journey was guided by divine love.

CHAPTER 11

Preparing for Parenthood

The months leading up to the twins' arrival were filled with activity and anticipation. Corinne and Joshua busied themselves with preparations, transforming their home into a welcoming haven for their babies. They poured their hearts into every detail, from decorating the nursery to selecting baby essentials.

Corinne embraced the changes with enthusiasm and grace, while Joshua, despite his health challenges, remained a pillar of strength. His pacemaker, defibrillator, and lung disease were constant reminders of the hurdles they faced, but he approached each day with unwavering optimism and determination.

Every Saturday became a ritual of exploring baby stores, picking out cribs, onesies, and other necessities. They debated names, nursery themes, and their vision for the future. These moments of shared excitement deepened their bond and prepared them for the life they were about to embark upon.

Joshua's health was a concern, but he managed it with resilience and hope. His doctors were pleased with his progress, and Corinne was ever-vigilant in ensuring he took care of himself while joyfully planning for their twins.

One evening, as they sat in the nursery surrounded by baby gear, Corinne looked at Joshua with a tender smile. "Can you believe how close we are to meeting our little ones?"

Joshua took her hand, his eyes shining with love. "It feels like a dream. I can't wait to hold them and start this new chapter with you."

Their conversations often turned to their hopes for their children, and they found solace in knowing that their preparations were guided by faith. They prayed together, asking God to bless their growing family and grant them the strength to be loving and attentive parents.

"Lord," Corinne prayed one evening, her voice filled with gratitude, "we thank You for the blessings You've bestowed upon us. We trust in Your guidance and ask for Your continued presence in our lives as we prepare to welcome our babies."

Joshua nodded in agreement. "We give You all the glory, Lord. Thank You for this journey and for the gift of our children."

Their faith and love for each other were a beacon of light in their preparation, and they felt a profound sense of peace as they awaited the arrival of their twins.

CHAPTER 12

A New Beginning

The day of delivery arrived, bringing with it a whirlwind of emotions for Corinne and Joshua. As Corinne's labor began, Joshua remained a steadfast and calming presence, despite the concerns about his own health. The delivery room was a flurry of activity as medical staff prepared for the arrival of the twins.

Corinne, surrounded by a supportive medical team, felt a deep sense of peace knowing Joshua was by her side. Despite the pain, she was comforted by his reassuring presence and the love they shared.

After hours of labor, the moment of joy came. The cries of the twins filled the room, and Joshua's eyes filled with tears as he held his newborn children for the first time. The sight of their tiny faces was a miracle he had longed for, a testament to the power of faith and perseverance.

The hospital room was soon filled with the warm presence of family and friends. Memo and Papa, beaming with pride, joined in the celebration of the twins' arrival. Corinne's parents and close friends also gathered to share in the joy.

Joshua looked at Corinne, his heart overflowing with love and gratitude. "We did it, Cori. They're finally here."

Corinne, exhausted but radiant, nodded with a joyful smile. "Yes, we did. Our family is complete."

As they welcomed their twins into the world, Corinne and Joshua knew that their journey was marked by divine blessings. Their faith had guided them through challenges, and they were ready to embrace the new chapter of parenthood with open hearts.

CHAPTER 13

Home Sweet Home

Bringing the twins home was a momentous occasion, filled with a mix of excitement and trepidation. The nursery, once a vision, was now a vibrant and welcoming space for their babies. Corinne and Joshua settled into their new routine, adjusting to the demands of parenthood while cherishing every precious moment.

Family and friends visited regularly, their support providing comfort and encouragement. Joshua's health remained a factor, but his dedication to being a loving father never wavered. Corinne's support was unwavering, and together they navigated the joys and challenges of raising twins.

One evening, as they sat together with their sleeping babies, Corinne and Joshua reflected on their journey. The challenges they had faced only made their triumphs more meaningful, and their faith continued to be a guiding force.

"This is what we've always dreamed of," Corinne said softly, leaning her head on Joshua's shoulder. "Our family is finally here."

Joshua kissed her forehead, his heart full. "Yes, and we've made it through everything together. I couldn't have asked for a better partner."

Their conversations often turned to their hopes and dreams for their children. They found comfort in knowing they were building a loving and supportive home, and their faith in God provided strength and guidance.

"Lord," Joshua prayed quietly as they sat together, "we thank You for the gift of our children and for the strength You've given us. We pray that You continue to guide us as we raise them in Your love."

Corinne nodded in agreement. "We give You all the glory and praise, Lord. Thank You for this beautiful journey."

Their faith remained a cornerstone of their family life, guiding them through each day with hope and gratitude.

CHAPTER 14

The Growing Family

As the twins grew, so did their bond as a family. Joshua and Corinne embraced their roles as parents with dedication, balancing the joys and challenges of raising two babies. Their home was filled with laughter, love, and the occasional sleepless night.

Family gatherings became cherished events, with Memo and Papa regularly visiting to spend time with their great-grandchildren. The twins thrived in the loving environment, and their milestones were celebrated with great joy.

Memo's face lit up every time she saw her great-grandchildren. She delighted in telling stories from the past and sharing her wisdom and love. Papa, ever the jester, entertained the twins with his playful antics, creating memories that would last a lifetime.

One day, as they watched the twins play in the living room, Corinne turned to Joshua with a smile. "Look at them. They're growing so fast."

Joshua wrapped his arm around her, his eyes reflecting pride and love. "I know. It's amazing to see them flourish. And we've come so far together."

Memo and Papa often joined Corinne and Joshua in their home, bringing a sense of continuity and tradition to the family. They marveled at how their great-grandchildren were growing and took immense joy in watching them reach new milestones.

During one of their visits, Memo sat with the twins on her lap, her eyes twinkling with affection. "These little ones are the light of our lives," she said, her voice filled with emotion. "I'm so grateful to see them growing up surrounded by love."

Papa nodded in agreement, his eyes moist with pride. "They're a blessing, that's for sure. I'm proud of you two for the wonderful parents you've become."

Joshua and Corinne's conversations often turned to their hopes for their children's future. They found comfort in knowing that their faith was guiding them through the challenges of parenthood. They prayed together for wisdom, strength, and continued blessings.

"Lord," Corinne prayed one evening, "we thank You for the joy our children bring and for the strength You provide us. We ask for Your continued guidance as we raise them in Your love."

Joshua nodded in agreement. "We give You all the glory, Lord. Thank You for this incredible journey."

Their faith remained a guiding light, and they continued to build a loving and supportive home for their growing family. The presence of Memo and Papa added an extra layer of richness to their lives, a reminder of the legacy of love and faith that had been passed down through the generations.

CHAPTER 15

New Beginnings and Everlasting Faith

The arrival of the twins brought profound changes to Joshua and Corinne's lives, weaving a new chapter into their love story. The days were filled with the sweet sounds of baby giggles and the challenges of sleepless nights, but every moment was cherished. Their home had transformed into a haven of joy and laughter.

As the twins grew, so did their bond with each other and their parents. Joshua and Corinne, now seasoned parents, embraced every new milestone with gratitude. Their hearts were full as they watched their children take their first steps, speak their first words, and experience the world with wonder.

One crisp autumn afternoon, Joshua and Corinne decided to take the twins for a stroll in the park. The leaves had turned brilliant shades of red and gold, and the cool breeze was invigorating. The twins giggled as they saw the falling leaves, their tiny hands reaching out to catch them.

Joshua pushed the stroller with a steady rhythm, his heart swelling with love. He glanced over at Corinne, who was beaming with joy.

"Look at them," he said softly. "They're growing so fast. I can't believe how blessed we are."

Corinne nodded, her eyes filled with tears of happiness. "I know. Every day feels like a gift. I thank God for bringing us together and for the family we've built."

Their stroll led them to a quiet spot under a large oak tree. Joshua stopped the stroller and took Corinne's hand. "Let's pray," he suggested, his voice filled with reverence. "We need to give thanks for all these blessings."

They knelt on the grass, the twins watching curiously from their stroller. Joshua began to pray, his heart full of gratitude. "Heavenly Father, we come before You with hearts full of thanks. Thank You for the gift of our children, for the love and strength You've given us, and for the joy we experience every day. We ask for Your continued guidance as we raise these precious little ones. May they grow in Your love and grace."

Corinne added her voice, "Lord, we give You all the glory for the blessings in our lives. We pray for wisdom and patience as parents and for health and happiness for our family. We trust in Your plan and know that with Your love, we can face any challenge."

As they finished their prayer, Joshua and Corinne looked at each other with a deep sense of peace. Their faith had been their anchor through every trial and joy, and they knew that it would continue to guide them.

In the coming months, life continued to unfold with new experiences and milestones. The twins reached their first birthdays, celebrated with a joyful party surrounded by family and friends. Memo and Papa beamed with pride as they held their great-grandchildren, their hearts overflowing with love.

Joshua and Corinne continued to nurture their faith, attending church regularly and sharing their journey with their community. They found strength in their spiritual family and joy in serving others, always giving glory to God for the blessings they had received.

One Sunday morning, as the congregation sang hymns of praise, Joshua and Corinne looked around at their church family. They felt a profound sense of belonging and gratitude. Their hearts were full as they reflected on the journey that had brought them to this moment.

Joshua squeezed Corinne's hand, his eyes meeting hers with a smile. "We've come a long way, haven't we?"

Corinne nodded, her eyes shining with tears of joy. "Yes, and we've done it with God's grace and love guiding us every step of the way."

As the final hymn played, Joshua and Corinne stood together, holding their twins close. They gave thanks for the love and support of their family, for the strength they found in their faith, and for the beautiful future that lay ahead.

Their story was one of love, faith, and perseverance, a testament to the power of God's grace in their lives. They knew that no matter what the future held, they would face it together, with hearts full of gratitude and a deep trust in the Lord.